Heart's DelighT
NINE-PATCH VARIATIONS

by
Patricia Knoechel

General information to review for all projects.

List of supplies

- Use 100% cotton fabrics 45" wide
- Use thin bonded batting for machine quilting
- Industrial size rotary cutter with fresh blade
- Gridded cutting mat 17" x 23"
- Plexiglass rulers: 6" x 12", 6" x 24", 12 1/2" Square Up
- Small safety pins, about 100 for larger projects
- Walking foot or Even-feed foot sewing machine attachment
- Neutral thread for general sewing
- Invisible thread or thread to match the 9-patch chain
- Craft supplies: see wreath

Projects with hearts

- Template plastic for tracing heart pattern
- Sewing machine blind hem or zig-zag stitch for applique, and invisible thread
- Thread to match the hearts if hand appliqued

General cutting and sewing instructions

fold

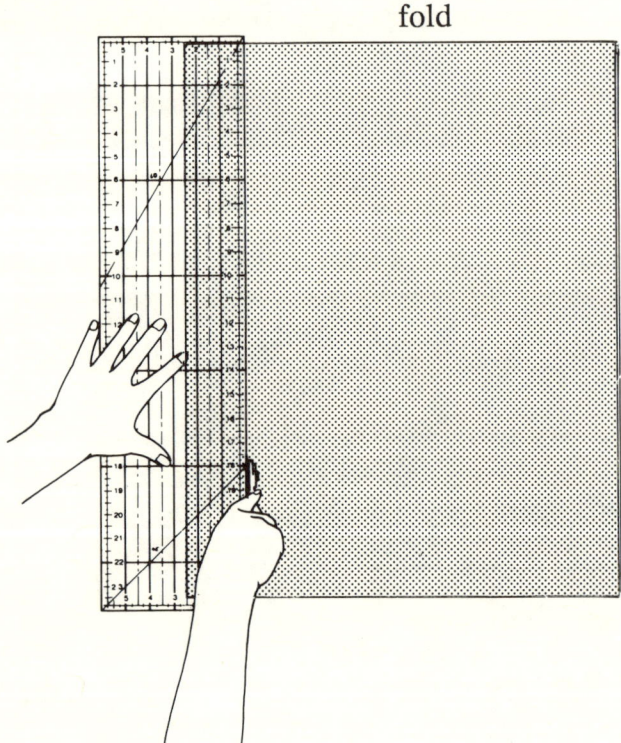

Instructions for cutting strips selvage to selvage: Accuracy is important! Fold the 45" wide fabric once and lay on gridded cutting mat. Lay plexiglass ruler on raw edges and rotary cut, trimming for a clean, straight edge. Move ruler over to desired strip width and cut.

Instructions for cutting border stripe fabric: When cutting border strips from a border stripe fabric, cut each strip separately, one layer, the length of the stripe. One yard of fabric will give you strips 36" long.

Sew a 1/4" seam allowance and 12 to 15 stitches to the inch, or a #2 on machines ranging from 1 to 4.

Assembly-line sewing refers to continuously sewing, butting one set after another without cutting the connecting thread.

Back-stitching at the start or end of seam is usually unnecessary because another seam will cross it.

"Stitching in the ditch" is machine quilting into a seam line.

Finishing the quilt instructions are given in detail in the first project, Mini Heart Wallhanging. Refer to these same details for finishing the other quilt projects. Similarly, later projects will refer to others by page number for a same procedure.

Yardage and cutting requirements are included at the beginning of each project.

Mini Heart Wallhanging

Approximately 28" Square

Materials Needed:		Cut:
1/3 yd Dark Fabric	**Nine-Patch**	1 strip 2 1/2" x 45"
		1 strip 2 1/2" x 11"
	First Border	2 strips 2 1/2" x 45"
1/3 yd Light Fabric	**Nine-Patch**	1 strip 2 1/2" x 45"
	Heart Background	5 light fabric squares, Cut later
1/2 yd Large Floral Print **OR** 1 yd Border Stripe Fabric with 4 repeats	**Second Border Fabric Choices**	3 strips 4 1/2" x 45" **OR** Cut four 36" strips approximately 4 1/2" wide, parallel with selvage
5/8 yd Medium Fabric	**Binding**	3 strips 3" x 45"
	Hearts	2 strips 4 1/2" x 45"
1 yd Muslin	**Backing**	
1 yd Lightweight	**Batting**	

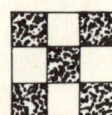

Making the 4 Nine-Patches

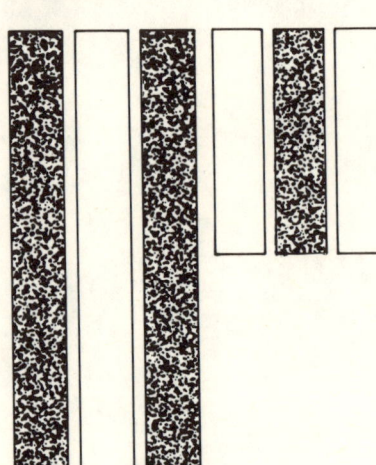

1. Count out
   one dark strip 2 1/2" x 45",
   one dark strip 2 1/2" x 11", and
   one light strip 2 1/2" x 45".

2. Cut the 45" dark strip in half,
   making two 2 1/2" x 22" strips.
   Repeat with the light strip.

3. Lay out two 22" dark strips and
   one 22" light strip. Cut the
   remaining 22" x 2 1/2" light
   strip in half, making two 11"
   strips. Lay out with the 11"
   dark strip.

4. Use an accurate 1/4" seam allowance for all sewing, and 12
   to 15 stitches per inch (or 2 on
   1-4). Sew the strips together.

5. On the back side, press the
   seams to the dark side. Then
   press again on the front side.

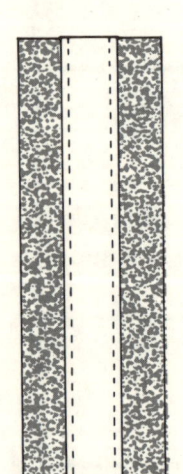
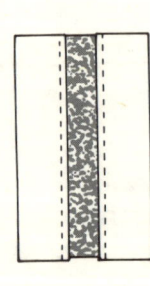

6. Position the 11" strip set on top
   of the 22" strip set right sides
   together. Carefully line up the
   two strips along the left edge
   with the seams interlocking.

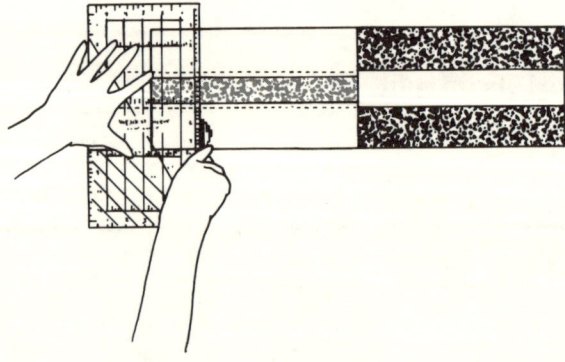

7. Square off the left end of the
   layered strips. Cut four 2 1/2"
   strips and stack the four pairs.
   They are now ready for sewing.
   Set aside.

8. Cut and stack four more 2 1/2"
   strips from the remaining strip
   set. Lay out the two stacks as illustrated.

9. Begin sewing the top pair of
   the paired stack.

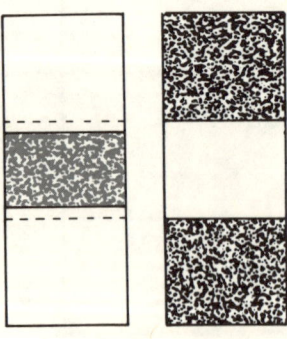

8 in stack   4 in stack

Finger pinning: Line up the first seams, interlocking with one seam up and the other seam down. Hold your finger over the seam as you approach it. Once sewn, line up the second seams, stretching to meet if necessary. Again place your finger over the second seam as it is approached.

10. Butt and assembly-line sew all four pairs in this manner. Do not stop to clip threads between each pair.

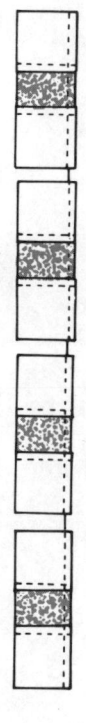

11. Continue assembly-line sewing the second stack of 2 1/2" strips along the right edge of the assembled pairs.

12. Press the blocks and measure the average size of each block. Depending on your seam allowance, the blocks will be approximately 6" to 6 1/2" square. For accurate assembly, square up the blocks, making them all the same size.

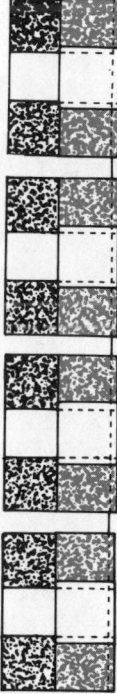

Making the 5 Heart Blocks

Cut a strip of background fabric the same width of your nine-patch measurement, approximately 6" to 6 1/2". Cut 5 background squares the same size as your completed nine-patch.

Making the Hearts

1. Trace the heart (page 7) from the pattern onto template plastic. Cut out shape.

2. Place the two 4 1/2" x 45" strips of heart fabric right sides together. Trace five hearts onto the wrong side of the layered heart fabric as illustrated. Allow 1/2" space between hearts. Cut apart, being careful to leave a seam allowance beyond the tracing line.

Appliqueing Hearts onto Background Squares

Choose one of the two applique methods given below.

Method A, Cheater's Applique with batting, is slightly more time consuming because it requires hand sewing. The advantage is that the hearts are more dimensional.

Method B, Invisible Applique, is time saving because the hearts are machine stitched onto the background with invisible thread.

Method A, Cheater's Applique with batting

1. Place a piece of lightweight batting behind each layered heart. Pin through all three thicknesses.

2. With 15 to 20 stitches per inch, stitch directly onto the tracing line of each heart. Stitch slowly around the curves to create a smoothly rounded edge. When necessary, lift the presser foot (with the needle down) and pivot the fabric.

3. Trim the seam to 1/8". Clip a V into the top center seam and bottom seam of each heart. On the fabric side (backing) of the heart carefully cut an opening in the center. To avoid cutting through both fabric layers, start the incision with a seam ripper by gently pushing the point of the ripper into the fabric. Lift to separate the two layers of fabric.

4. With scissors, cut a small heart shaped opening from the backing. Turn right side out. To round out the edge, finger press by running the seam between your thumb and index finger.

5. To find the center of the background squares, fold in half and crease lightly with your finger. Line up the center of the heart with the crease. Pin in place by inserting pins through the seam along the outside edge. Blindstitch by hand, catching the backing layer of the heart with the background fabric.

Method B - Invisible Applique

Follow the preceding method without the additional layer of batting. Instead of handstitching the heart to the background, machine stitch with invisible thread as follows: Use regular thread to match the heart in your bobbin and feed the invisible thread on top through a thread stand. Set the tension on 1 or 2 and set the stitch on blind hem or zig-zag. Stitch close to the heart on the background and catch the heart with the zig-zag as illustrated.

Stitching and Tracing Line

Making template from Heart Pattern
Trace the heart onto template plastic. Cut out shape with old scissors.

Sewing the Blocks Together

1. Lay out the nine squares as illustrated.

2. Sew vertical seams first, using the assembly-line method as illustrated. Do not clip the rows apart.

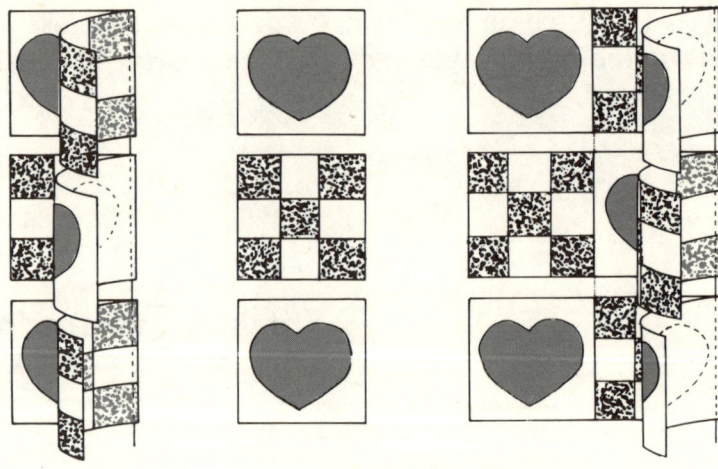

3. Sew horizontal seams. Where two seams meet, push one seam up and the other seam down. Press the quilt.

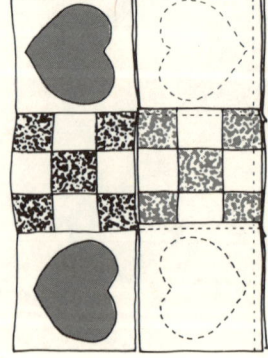

Adding the Borders

First Border

Square off the ends of both 2 1/2" x 45" dark strips. Line up a strip, right sides together with one edge of the quilt and stitch. Open and press. Square off the excess strip. Repeat the border on the opposite side. Open, press and trim excess. Then add two borders to the two remaining sides.

Square all four corners with a Square Up ruler and rotary cutter.

Second Border Option of Floral Print

three 4 1/2" x 45" strips (selvage to selvage)

Add the second border in the same manner as the first border. Cut one strip in half for the two shorter sides.

OR

Second Border Option of Border Stripe with Mitered Corner

four 4 1/2" x 36" strips (parallel with selvage)

This option uses four border stripes 4 1/2" x 36" long. The length of each border should include the length of the side of the quilt plus two times the width of the stripe plus 3" to 5" extra for matching the pattern at the mitered corners.

With right sides together, line up two borders on two opposite sides at the quilt top. If the border stripe has a geometric design, **center and match** the pattern from side to side in order to make the design meet at the corner miter. Pin in place and stitch, starting and stopping 1/4" in from each edge. Backstitch at each end. The strips extend beyond the quilt.

Press out the two borders and add the two remaining borders in the same manner. These strips also extend beyond the quilt.

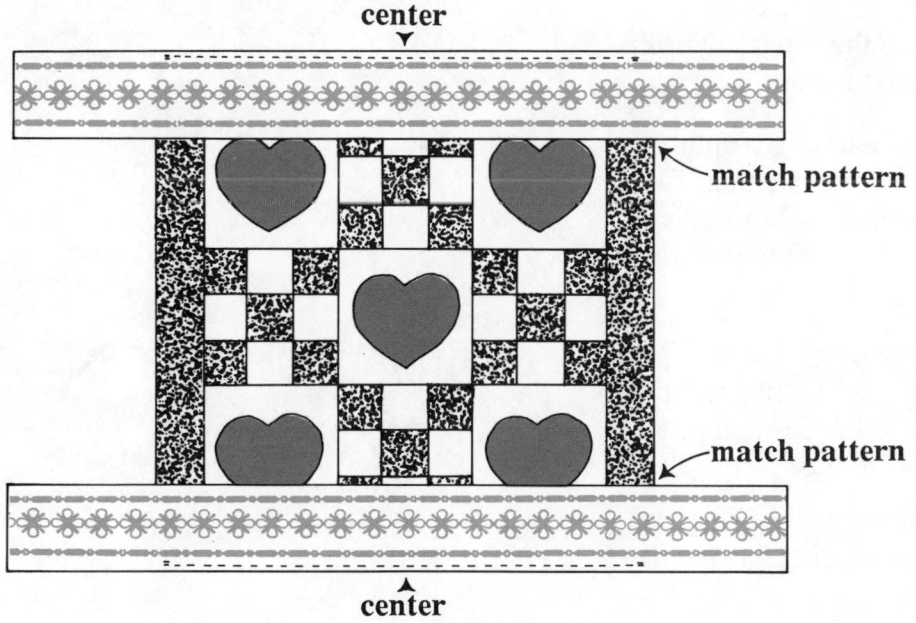

Mitering the Corner

At the ironing board as you press out the two final borders, press in a diagonal crease as follows: Diagonally fold the top strip under and bring the two ends together as shown. If the border stripe has dominant lines in the pattern, match up the lines from both borders and press in place. From the wrong side of the fabric, pin the strips together matching up the lines at the diagonal crease. Following along the creased diagonal line, begin stitching from the outside edge to the inside edge. Trim the seams to 1/2" and press open.

Machine Quilting

If desired, first mark your stitching lines with a quilter's silver or white pencil. Draw diagonally through the chain of dark connecting squares.

1. Lay out the muslin backing, or printed fabric right side down. Place the batting on top of the backing. Center the quilt top onto the batting.

2. With small safety pins, pin together the three layers of fabric every 4" to 5". Do not pin on the chains (dark connecting squares) where the stitching will be.

3. When machine quilting, a walking foot will prevent fabric shifting and puckering. Thread should be invisible or match the dark fabric. Use 10 stitches per inch or set on #3 when stitching through batting.

4. First stitch through the blocks in the directions of the arrows. Then "stitch in the ditch" on both sides of the first border.

5. If desired, sew a casing strip on the top edge of the backing. To hang, slip a dowel rod through the casing and set the ends on push pins.

6. To stabilize the outside edge while adding the binding, smooth out the outside border and pin in place every 4" to 5".

Do not trim the excess backing and batting until the binding has been added.

Adding the Binding

1. Square the ends of the strips, removing selvages. Sew together the three 3" x 45" strips to make a long continuous strip. Press the strip in half widthwise with the right sides out.

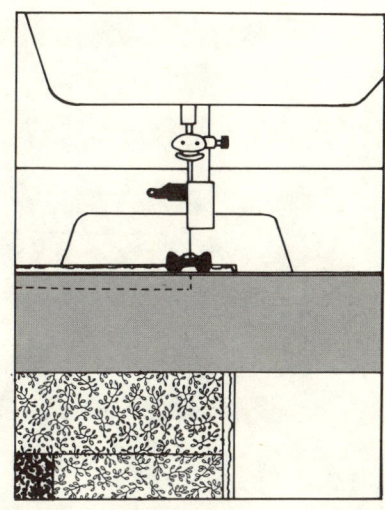

2. Starting at the center of one side of the quilt, line up the raw edges of the binding with the raw edges of the quilt top. Begin stitching, leaving the first 4" of the binding to hang free. Use 1/4" seam allowance.

3. As you approach a corner, stop stitching 1/4" from the edge. With the needle down, pivot the quilt as you would to turn the corner. Instead of sewing forward, backstitch to the edge of the border. Lift the presser foot and pull the quilt slightly towards you.

4. Fold the binding straight up towards the needle, making a 45° fold.

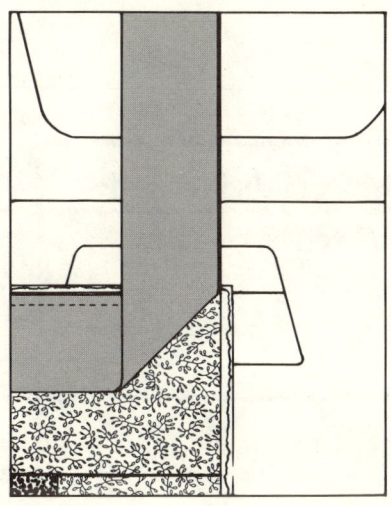

5. Then fold the binding straight down as illustrated. Line up the raw edge of the binding with the next side of the quilt. Continue stitching. Miter each corner in the same manner.

6. As you approach the starting point, stop stitching about 8" before the beginning stitches. Lay the two ends of the binding flat along the edge of the quilt. Trim, so that one strip overlaps the second strip by 1/2". Unfold and stitch the two ends together in a 1/4" seam.

7. Fingerpress the seam open. Finish stitching the binding to the quilt. Trim the batting and backing to 1/8".

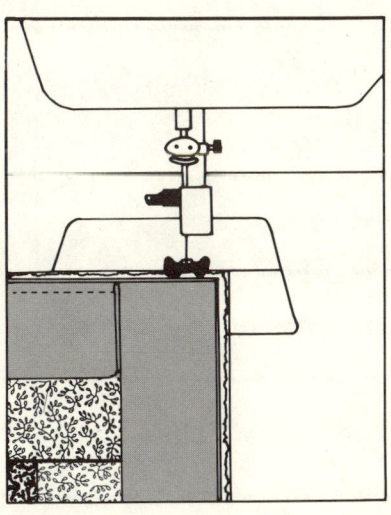

8. Wrap the binding around to the back of the quilt. Line up the folded edge of the binding with the stitching line. Pin in place and blindstitch by hand. At each corner make a tuck behind each miter. To avoid bulk, turn the tuck in the direction opposite the miter on top.

Four Blocks with Bouquet

Diagonal Set

Approximately 27" Square

Materials Needed:		Cut:	
1/2 yd Dark Fabric	**Nine-Patch**	1 strip 2 1/2" x 45"	
		1 strip 2 1/2" x 11"	
	Binding	3 strips 3" x 45"	
1/2 yd Light Fabric	**Nine-Patch**	1 strip 2 1/2" x 45"	
	Background	Cut later	
1/4 yd Medium Fabric	**First Border**	2 strips 2 1/2" x 45"	
1/2 yd Floral Print * **OR** 1 yd Border Stripe Fabric with 4 repeats	**Second Border Fabric Choices**	3 strips 4 1/2" x 45" **OR** Cut four 36" strips approximately 4 1/2" wide, parallel with selvage	
1 yd Muslin	**Backing**		
1 yd Lightweight	**Batting**		

* Note: If using large floral grouping for center square as shown in photograph, purchase 5/8 yd fabric. Do not cut borders until later.

Making the 4 Nine-Patches

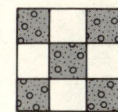

Follow the assembly method for making the 4 nine-patches as described in the Mini Heart Wallhanging on pages 4 and 5.

Cutting the Background Pieces

Side Triangles

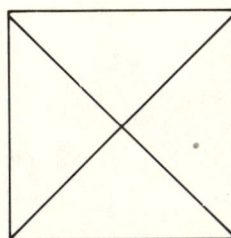

To calculate the measurement for the side triangles, first measure the length of the diagonal between two opposite corners of your nine-patch block. Then add 5/8" to this figure.

For example, a 6 1/4" nine-patch block measures 8 7/8" diagonally. With an additional 5/8", the calculated size is 9 1/2".

Cut one light square to your calculated size. (Measurement of diagonal plus 5/8") Cut diagonally into four triangles.

Corner Triangles

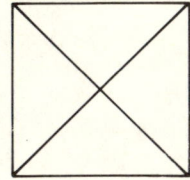

Cut one light square to your block size plus 1". For example, 6 1/4" plus 1" equals 7 1/4". Cut diagonally into four triangles.

Center Square

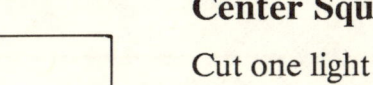

Cut one light square the same size as your nine-patch blocks.

If your choice was a floral center, cut from floral fabric being careful to reserve enough for border.

Sewing the Blocks Together

Lay out the nine-patch blocks with the background pieces in diagonal rows.

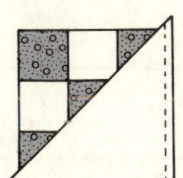

When sewing a triangle to a square, line up the square ends and allow the tips to extend 3/8". Be very careful not to stretch the bias edges of the triangles. Pin and sew in diagonal rows.

Sew the rows together matching the seams with one seam up, and the other seam down. Press the quilt.

Finishing the Quilt

Finish the borders, backing, machine quilting and binding following the Mini Heart instructions starting on page 9.
Machine quilting will be horizontal and vertical rather than on the diagonal.

Amish Wallhanging

Approximately 44" Square

Note: Refer to the color photograph on the inside back cover for the positioning of the colors.

Materials Needed:		Cut:
3/4 yd Magenta Fabric	**Nine-Patch**	5 strips 2 1/2" x 45"
	Binding	4 strips 3" x 45"
1 yd Black Fabric	**Nine-Patch**	4 strips 2 1/2" x 45"
	Second Border	4 strips 5" x 45"
2/3 yd Dark Blue Fabric	**Background**	Cut later
	Border Corner Squares	4 squares 5"
1/2 yd Med Blue Fabric	**Second Background**	Cut 4 squares later
	First Border	4 strips 2" x 45"
1 3/8 yds Muslin	**Backing**	
1 1/4 yds Lightweight	**Batting**	

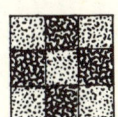

Making the 16 Nine-Patch Blocks

Making the Strip Sets

1. Count out five 2 1/2" magenta strips and four 2 1/2" black strips.

2. Lay out the 45" strips into three sets as illustrated.

3. Sew the strip sets together to make two magenta - black - magenta strip sets and one black - magenta - black strip set.

4. On the back side, press the seams to the black side. Then press again on the front side.

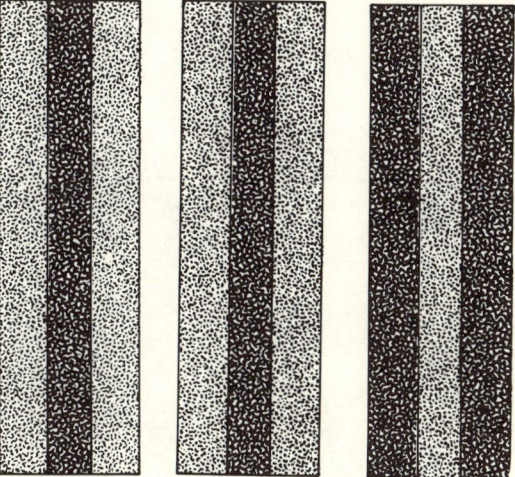

Cutting the 2 1/2" Strips for the Nine-Patch Blocks

1. Position the black - magenta - black strip set on top of a magenta - black - magenta strip set right sides together. Carefully line up the two sets with the seams interlocking to prevent fabric shifting while layer cutting.

2. Square off the left end of the layered strips. Cut sixteen 2 1/2" strips and stack the pairs. They are now ready for sewing. Set aside.

3. From the remaining magenta - black - magenta set, cut sixteen 2 1/2" strips. Lay out this stack with the paired stack as illustrated.

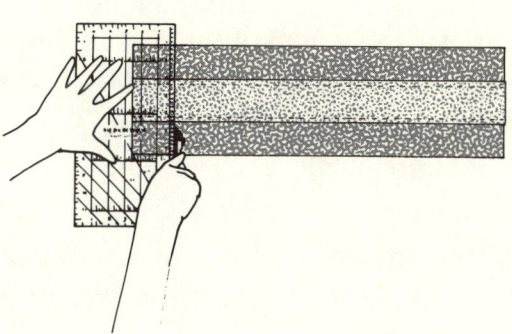

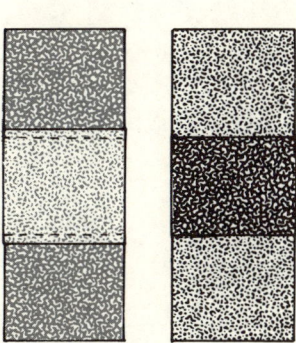

32 in stack   16 in stack

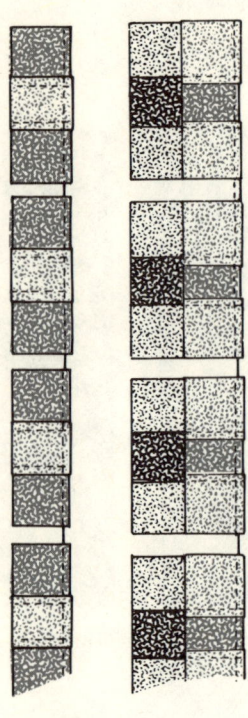

Assembly-line Sewing All 16 Blocks

1. Begin by sewing the top pair in the paired stack. Fingerpin by lining up the first seams interlocking with one seam up and the other seam down. Hold your finger over the seam as you approach it. Once sewn, line up the second seams, stretching to meet if necessary. Again place your finger over the second seam as you approach it.

2. Once you have stitched the first pair, continue with the remaining pairs in the assembly-line method.

3. Assembly-line sew the second stack of 2 1/2" strips along the right edge of the assembled pairs to form the nine-patch blocks.

4. Press your blocks and measure the average size of each block. Depending on your seam allowance, the blocks will be approximately 6" to 6 1/2" square. For accurate assembly, square up your blocks, making them all the same size.

Cutting the Background Pieces

Side Triangles

To calculate the measurement for the side triangles, first measure the length of the diagonal between two opposite corners of your nine-patch block. Then add 5/8" to this figure.

For example a 6 1/4" block measures 8 7/8" diagonally. With an additional 5/8", the calculated size is 9 1/2".

Using the Main Background Fabric, **cut three squares** to your calculated size. (Measurement of diagonal plus 5/8") Cut each diagonally into four triangles for a total of 12 side triangles.

Corner Triangles

Using the Main Background Fabric, **cut one square** the size of your block plus 1". For example, 6 1/4" plus 1" equals 7 1/4". Cut diagonally into four triangles for the corners of your quilt.

Background Squares

You need a **total of nine background squares** cut the same size as your nine-patch blocks. As shown in the color photograph of the Amish quilt, cut **five** of these squares in your Main Background Fabric. Cut the other **four** squares from your Second Background Fabric.

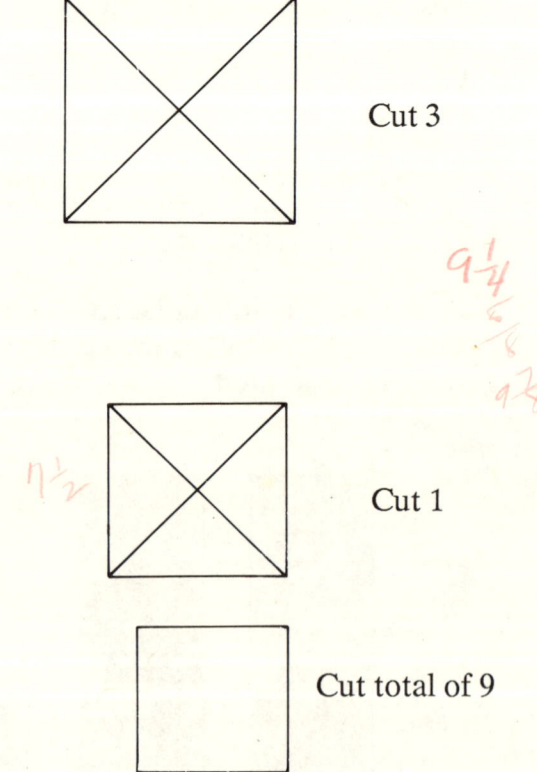

Cut 3

Cut 1

Cut total of 9

Sewing the Blocks Together

Lay out the nine-patch blocks with the background pieces in diagonal rows.

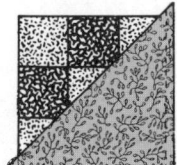 When sewing a triangle to a square, line up the square ends and allow the tips to extend 3/8". Be very careful not to stretch the bias edges of the triangles. Pin and sew in diagonal rows.

Sew the rows together matching the seams with one seam up, and the other seam down. Press the quilt top.

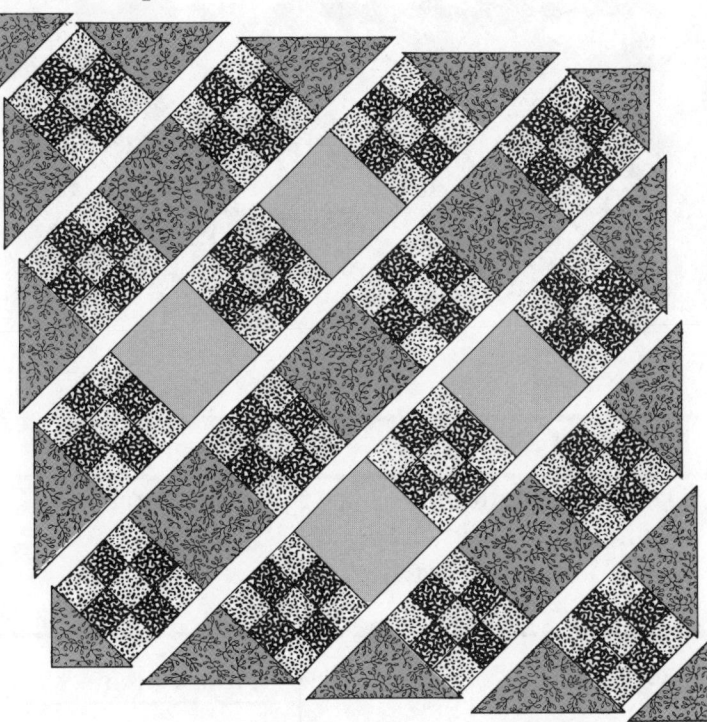

Adding the Borders

First Border

Using the four 2" x 45" first border strips, sew to the quilt top as in Mini Heart first border on page 9.

Second Border

1. Measure the length of the quilt across the center with the first border added. Cut 4 strips at that measurement from the 5" x 45" second border strips.

2. Sew two border strips to opposite sides of quilt.

3. Add a 5" border corner square to each end of the remaining two border strips.

4. Matching the seams, pin and sew the final border strips to the quilt. Press the quilt.

Finishing the Quilt

Layer the quilt with batting and backing, and finish the quilt following the Mini Heart Wallhanging instructions on page 10. Start with Machine Quilting. Machine quilting will be horizontal and vertical rather than on the diagonal.

Old Fashioned Scrap Quilt or Baby Quilt

Approximately 44" Square

Materials Needed:		**Cut:**
Darks and Mediums 20 different fabric scraps, or use some fabrics twice.	**Nine-Patch**	20 strips 2 1/2" x 10 1/2" Must be cut accurately. Remove all selvages.
1 yd Light at least 44" wide	**Nine-Patch**	4 strips 2 1/2" x 45"
	Background	Cut later
1/8 yd Medium or scraps	**Optional 4 Hearts**	
1/3 yd Dark Fabric	**First Border**	4 strips 2" x 45"
5/8 yd Floral Print	**Second Border**	4 strips 5" x 45"
3/8 yd Light or Dark	**Binding**	4 strips 3" x 45"
1 3/8 yds Muslin	**Backing**	
1 1/2 yds Lightweight	**Batting**	

Making 16 Scrap Nine-Patch Blocks

Making Two Scrap - Light - Scrap Strip Sets

1. It is important that the 20 scrap pieces be exactly 10 1/2" long and have all selvages removed. Count out eight 2 1/2" x 10 1/2" scrap strips.

2. Square off one end of a light 2 1/2" x 45" strip. Position it right side up under sewing machine needle.

3. Right sides together, lay a scrap against the long light strip and sew the length of the scrap piece. Butt and stitch the second scrap behind the first. Continue with a third and fourth scrap strip, filling the long light strip.

4. Square off the end of the light strip even with the last scrap strip.

5. Starting with this squared off end, add four more strips to the opposite side of the light strip, lifting the scrap strips out of the way.

6. Make a second strip set in the same manner as the first.

7. On the back side, press the seams to the dark side. Then press again on the front side.

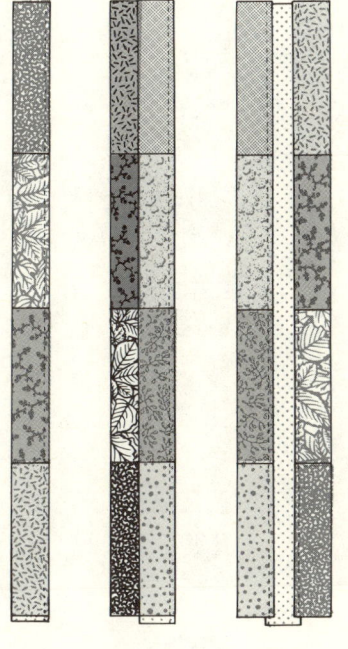

Making One Light - Scrap - Light Strip Set

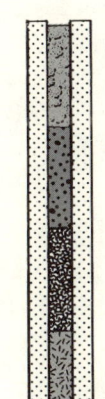

1. Count out two 2 1/2" x 45" light strips, and four 2 1/2" x 10 1/2" scrap strips.

2. Square off one end of a light strip and sew four scrap strips as done in the previous strip sets. Square off the end.

3. Square off the second light strip and position under the sewing machine needle. Beginning with the last scrap strip added, place right sides together with the second light strip. Stitch and butt the remaining scrap strips. Square off the end.

4. From the back side, press the seams to the dark side. Then press again from the front side.

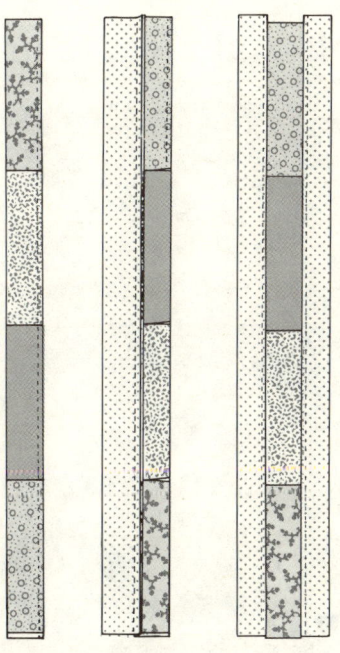

Cutting 2 1/2" Strips for the Nine-Patch Blocks

Each of the three strip sets will make sixteen 2 1/2" strips. Cut one strip at a time as follows:

Square off the left end of the strip set. Cut four 2 1/2" strips from each 10 1/2" scrap strip set. Begin each 10 1/2" section by squaring off the left edge.

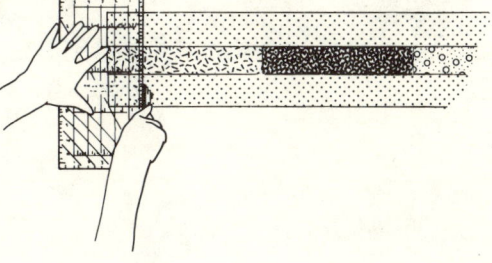

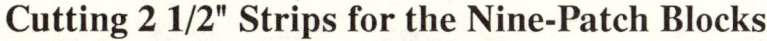

19

Assembly-line Sewing All 16 Blocks

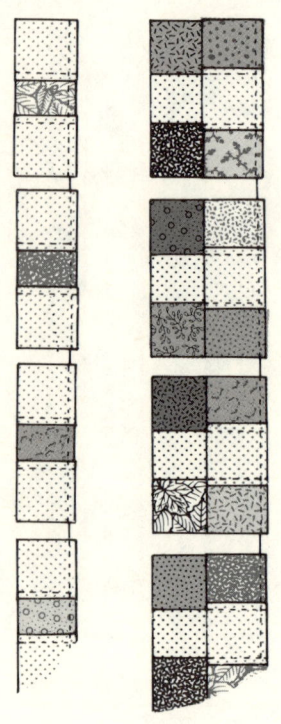

1. Randomize the Fabric: Once sixteen pieces have been cut, place them in a brown paper bag. Shake and toss, then stack the pieces. Make three stacks from the three strip sets.

2. Arrange the three stacks with the light - scrap - light (B) stack in the middle.

3. Set aside the (A) stack on the right and place the first two stacks next to your sewing machine.

4. Pick up the piece on top of each stack. Place piece B on top of piece A. Stitch as illustrated matching the seams.

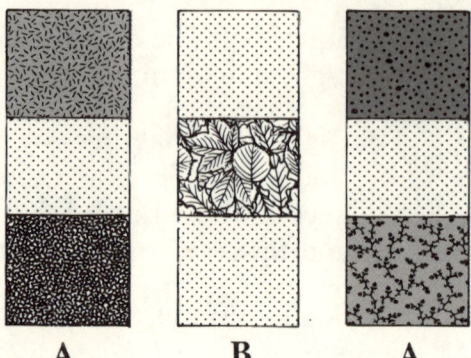

A   B   A

5. Once you have stitched the first two pieces together, do not stop to lift your presser foot or clip the threads. Butt the second pair of pieces behind the first. Continue with the remaining pieces in this assembly-line method.

6. Now take the third stack of pieces (A) and sew them along the right edge of the AB pieces. Use the assembly-line method as described in the preceding step.

Optional Hearts on four Background Squares

1. Make template plastic heart from pattern on page 7.

2. Fold the 1/8 yd heart fabric in half lengthwise, right sides together.

3. Following the instructions for either applique method A or B, starting on page 6, applique four hearts on four background squares which are cut in the next step.

   In order to center the heart on the square, fold and crease the square on the diagonal.

Adding the Background and Sewing the Blocks Together

To cut the background pieces and sew together the blocks, follow the instructions for the Amish quilt on page 16. Begin with "Cutting the Background Pieces" through "Sewing the Blocks Together."

Adding the Borders

First Border

Using the four 2" x 45" first border strips, sew to the quilt top as in Mini Heart first border on page 9.

Second Border

1. Measure the length of the quilt across the center including the first border. Using this measurement, cut two second border 5" strips. Pin the two strips to opposite sides of the quilt and sew.

2. Open and press the borders. Measure the two remaining sides including the newly added borders. Cut two border strips at that measurement, pin to quilt and sew. Press the quilt.

Finishing the Quilt

Layer the quilt with batting and backing, and finish the quilt following the Mini Heart Wallhanging instructions on page 10. Start with Machine Quilting. Machine quilting will be horizontal and vertical rather than on the diagonal.

Heart's Delight Wreath
Approximately 14" x 20"

Materials Needed:	Cut:
1/8 yd each of Four Heart Fabrics	Four 4 1/2" x 6" from each fabric
1/4 yd Bow Fabric	One 6" x 19" rectangle One 4 1/2" x 20" rectangle
1/3 yd Lightweight Batting	Eight 4 1/2" x 6" One 2 1/4" x 20" One 6" x 9 1/2"
12" Round Wire Wreath from Craft Supplier	
Fiberfill for Stuffing Hearts	
Hot Glue Gun	
Dried Baby's Breath or Status	
Optional: Dried Flowers	

Making the Eight Stuffed Hearts

1. Make template plastic heart from pattern on page 7.

2. For each of the eight hearts, place two 4 1/2" x 6" heart fabrics right sides together. Trace shape onto each layered rectangle.

3. Place a piece of batting under each layered heart and pin through all thicknesses.

4. To sew and turn the hearts, use the Cheater's Applique technique described starting on page 6.

Note: Instead of cutting a heart shaped opening in the back, simply cut a 2" slit. Turn and stuff the hearts with fiberfill. Whipstitch the openings.

Making the Bow

1. Fold the 6" x 19" rectangle in half, right side in, making it 6" x 9 1/2".

2. Fold the 4 1/2" x 20" rectangle in half, right side in, making it 2 1/4" x 20".

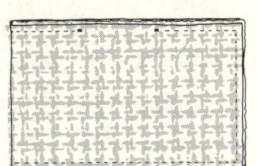
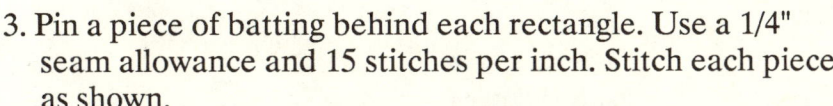
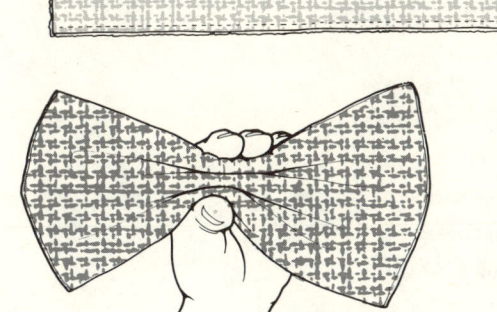

3. Pin a piece of batting behind each rectangle. Use a 1/4" seam allowance and 15 stitches per inch. Stitch each piece as shown.

4. Clip the corners and turn each piece right side out.

5. On the wider rectangle, hand pleat through the center and hold in place with left hand. Fold a tuck in the center of the long strip and then wrap it over the center of the bow. Machine stitch as illustrated.

Hot Gluing

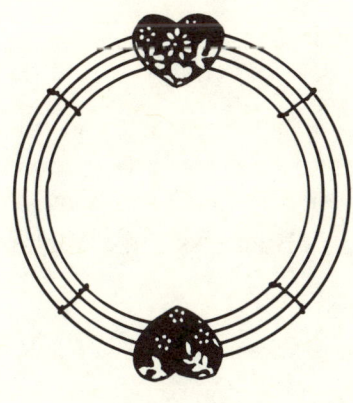

1. To center the hearts onto the wire wreath, note the positioning of the cross wires on your wreath. Hot glue two identical hearts at two opposite cross wires. Aim the glue onto the wire wreath and position each heart with the points turned into the center of the wreath.

2. Center two more identical hearts between the first two hearts. Fill in the remaining hearts.

3. Hot glue the ends of the bow and wrap around the wire. Trim off excess fabric.

4. To cover up the exposed wire, fill in with dried weeds and flowers.

   Additional Suggestion: Make a Victorian wreath with satins and lace. Embellish with ribbons and buttons.

Order Information:

If you do not have a fine quilt shop in your area, you may write for a complete catalog and current price list of all books and patterns published by Quilt in a Day®

Books

Quilt in a Day Log Cabin
The Sampler -- A Machine Sewn Quilt
Trio of Treasured Quilts
Lover's Knot Quilt
Amish Quilt in a Day
Irish Chain in a Day
Country Christmas
Bunnies and Blossoms
May Basket Quilt
Schoolhouse Wallhanging
Diamond Log Cabin Tablecloth or Treeskirt
Morning Star Quilt
Trip Around the World Quilt
Friendship Quilt
Creating With Color
Dresden Plate Quilt, a Simplified Method
Pineapple Quilt, a Piece of Cake
Radiant Star Quilt
Blazing Star Tablecloth

Booklets and Patterns

Patchwork Santa
Last Minute Gifts
Miniature May Basket
Dresden Plate Placemats and Tea Cozy
Angel of Antiquity
Log Cabin Wreath
Log Cabin Christmas Tree
Flying Geese Quilt
Miniature May Basket Wallhanging
Tulip Table Runner and Wall Hanging
Heart's Delight, Nine-Patch Variations

Supplies Available

Rotary Cutters
Rotary Replacement Blades
Cutting Mats with Grids
6" x 6" Mini Rulers
6" x 12" Rulers
6" x 24" Rulers
12 1/2" x 12 1/2" Square Up Rulers
Cutter Kits
Magnetic Pin Cushions
Invisible Threads
Bicycle Clips
Magnetic Seam Guides
Quilting Pins
Curved Needles
Pin Basting Kits
Fairfield Batting
T-Shirts

Videos for Rent or Purchase

Log Cabin
Ohio Star
Lover's Knot
Irish Chain
Schoolhouse Wallhanging
Diamond Log Cabin
Morning Star Quilt
Trip Around the World
Flying Geese
Block Party Series One Videos
Block Party Series Two Videos
and more!

If you are ever in Southern California, San Diego County, drop by and visit the Quilt in a Day Center. Our quilt shop and classroom is located in the La Costa Meadows Business Park. Write ahead for a current class schedule and map.

Quilt in a Day®
1955 Diamond Street, San Marcos, California 92069
Order Line: 1-800- U2 KWILT(1-800-825-9458)   Information Line: 1-619-591-0081